ANIMALS

Written by
Rod Barkman

GROSS NATURE

Gareth Stevens
PUBLISHING

Published in 2027 by
Gareth Stevens Publishing
2544 Clinton St.
Buffalo, NY 14224

Written by: Rod Barkman
Edited by: Beth Latham
Designed by: Ker Ker Lee

Cataloging-in-Publication Data
Names: Barkman, Rod.
Title: Animals / Rod Barkman.
Description: Buffalo, New York : Gareth Stevens Publishing, 2027. | Series: Gross nature | Includes glossary and index.
Identifiers: ISBN 9781482477801 (pbk.) | ISBN 9781482477818 (library bound) | ISBN 9781482477825 (ebook)
Subjects: LCSH: Animals--Juvenile literature. | Predatory animals--Juvenile literature. | Animal behavior--Juvenile literature.
Classification: LCC QL49.B37 2027 | DDC 590--dc23

Printed in China

CPSIA compliance information: Batch #QS27GS: For further information contact Gareth Stevens at 1-800-542-2595.

Photo Credits – Images courtesy of Shutterstock.com, unless otherwise stated.

Cover & Recurring – losw, Mott Jordan, Marloes Hermens, nicemonkey, WinWin artlab, Solodov Aleksei. 2–3 – As Arsyil. 4–5 – Stephen A. Waycott, Joe Belanger, Eric Isselee, Chanawat Jaiya. 6–7 – reptiles4all, Dan Olsen. 8–9 – Ishor gurung, KensCanning. 10–11 – Viktor Loki. 12–13 – Andrii Slonchak, Ethan Daniels. 14–15 – Michael Schroeder, Nick Pecker. 16–17 – Peter Southwood, CC BY-SA 4.0, via Wikimedia Commons, Bernard DUPONT from FRANCE, CC BY-SA 2.0, via Wikimedia Commons. 18–19 – SMontagud, johannviloria. 20–21 – Conservationist, RidhaAnshari. 22–23 – Henk Bogaard, David Havel, Ayman shalaby, Pressmaster.

CONTENTS

Words that look like <u>this</u> can be found in the glossary on page 24.

FOUL FACTS

There are millions of different animals in the world. Some are big, some are small, some are cute, and some are scary. Some of them are really, really gross.

Mosquito

Stargazer fish

This is a book about some of the most disgusting animals in the world. They come from the sea, the land, underground, and the air. Let's find out about some of the yuckiest animals in nature.

Naked mole-rat

SURINAM TOAD

The Surinam toad spends all its time in slow-moving water. The female toad lays eggs, which the male toad gently rubs into her back with his back legs. Then the gross part happens...

The mother toad's skin grows around the eggs. The baby toads hatch and live under her skin for months. When the time is right, holes open up on the female's back and the young toads pop out.

The skin of the female toad will grow around these eggs.

VULTURE

Most vultures are scavengers. This means that they do not hunt living animals. Instead, they eat animals that are already dead. Vultures are special because they can eat rotting food without getting sick.

Another word for dead animals is carrion.

Some vultures have no feathers on their heads and necks. This is useful when they stick their heads inside dead animals to eat. Bare skin is much easier to keep clean than feathers.

Some vultures also poop on themselves to cool down.

HORNED LIZARD

These lizards live in deserts. If a predator attacks, horned lizards can inflate their bodies to twice their size. Some horned lizards have an even more disgusting trick...

Horned lizards are named after the spikes on their heads.

Some horned lizards can shoot blood out of their eyes. The lizards can shoot the blood as far as 3 feet (1 m). The blood is also full of chemicals that are dangerous for predators such as dogs, wolves, and coyotes.

Shooting blood from the eyes confuses and scares predators.

SEA CUCUMBER

There are over 1,000 types of sea cucumbers in shallow and deep ocean waters. They crawl slowly along the seafloor, eating dead sea creatures and plankton. Plankton are tiny living things that float in the ocean.

Sea cucumbers do not have a brain.

Sea cucumbers are important for using and cleaning up waste in the sea. Some sea cucumbers escape predators by letting out a burst of waste. This quickly pushes them through the water.

Some sea cucumbers let out sticky white threads that trap other sea creatures.

NORTHERN FULMAR

These seabirds build their nests high up on cliffs. They lay a single egg and look after it for around 50 days until it hatches. But things start to get gross if a predator attacks.

Northern fulmars can live up to 50 years.

Northern fulmars can spit warm oil from their mouths. This stomach oil smells terrible and clogs up the wings of attackers. Sometimes, the parents feed this smelly stomach oil to their babies as food.

Northern fulmars can spit their warm oil over 3 feet (1 m) away.

Northern fulmar chick

HAGFISH

Hagfish live in cold water in oceans all over the world. They eat other fish, including fish that are already dead. They do this by burrowing into a dead body and eating their way out.

Hagfish are long and thin. They are soft fish with no scales.

When attacked, hagfish make a huge amount of slime. This comes out of tiny holes in their body. The slime clogs up the gills of predators, causing them to choke.

Hagfish slime is so thick that it can choke a shark.

BOMBARDIER BEETLE

Bombardier beetles are usually found among leaves on the ground or under stones. There are hundreds of different types of bombardier beetles. Some of them have a very yucky way of fighting predators...

Bombardier beetles live on every continent in the world except for Antarctica.

Some bombardier beetles can shoot stinky, boiling hot chemicals from their rear end. They shoot the chemicals in bursts—up to 500 a second. This stings a predator's eyes and lungs.

Bombardier beetles can aim their chemical spray and fire it in any direction.

SLOW LORIS

Slow lorises look very cute. However, they are also quite disgusting. Slow lorises have glands near their armpits that ooze toxins. After licking their armpits, they can give others a venomous bite.

Slow lorises live in trees.

Slow lorises have powerful jaws that can bite through bones. Their venom is powerful, too, and can melt the skin of other animals. However, slow lorises mainly use this venom on each other.

GROSS GOODBYE

Now you know how gross animals can be. Which animal do you think was the yuckiest? Do you know other gross animal facts?

Sea cucumber

If you could make your own gross animal, what body parts would you give it? Would it be an insect, a fish, a bird, or something else? Try drawing your animal. See how gross you can make it!

GLOSSARY

chemicals	matter that can be used to cause changes
continent	a large area of land, such as Africa or Europe, that is often made up of many countries
gills	the organs that some animals use to breathe underwater
glands	organs in the body that produce chemicals
hatch	when a baby animal comes out of an egg
predator	an animal that hunts other animals for food
rotting	when something is slowly breaking down, often going soft and smelly
toxins	substances that are harmful to people or the natural world
venomous	able to poison another animal through a bite or a scratch
waste	things left over that are no longer needed, such as poop or dead things

INDEX